Anton Davydov

**Harmonica Lessons
from Beginner to Advanced**

VIDEO
AND
AUDIO

Original Harmonica Method
of Learning to Play and Improvise

CONTENTS

PART III

Introduction

Hi there! It may sound a bit corny, but you are holding in your hands a unique book! Yes – unique! What's unique about it is that the teaching method shown here will teach you not only to hit the right notes and play melodies (you can learn this in many other books as well), but also to improvise. Yes, you heard that right – to improvise! And we will start doing it from the very first lessons. You think it's impossible? I'm sure many of you have already tried to master the harmonica (or the harp, as the players call it) by watching video lessons on the Internet or, perhaps, by other self-tutorial books. Perhaps you even got quite good at playing some melodies, but... it wasn't exactly what you set out to do – what you were ultimately striving for. You just wanted to pick up an instrument and play your own tune. Not someone else's, but your own melody - different, full of sorrow or joy. But you couldn't find a book that could teach you how to do that. Well, congratulations! If you're reading this, you've got exactly what you've been looking for.

Or maybe this is your first self-tutorial? Well, then you're in luck! In any case, let's not waste a minute and start our fascinating dive into one of the most marvelous worlds - the world of music.

By the way, let's get to know each other! Follow the qr-code *(Video 1)*.

Video 1*

*See page 64 for all videos and audio files.

To make our immersion into music successful and effective, we need to discuss and understand the principles of our training: the structure and the approach to mastering this marvelous musical instrument - harmonica.

There is a well-known idea that music is a language that is understood by all people on all continents. I couldn't agree more. In fact, we master playing a musical instrument in the same way as we learn to speak our native language. There are 5 basic principles to follow:

1. Listening more than playing.

This does not mean you should play little! It means you should emphasize listening more. If you haven't done so already, surround yourself with harmonica music. Let music come out of every device you have. On any music player, on the radio, in the car, at work (if you can), even on a vinyl record. What and who you will listen to is a matter of your taste. If you care about my opinion, I can give you a few names of outstanding harmonica players, who a good while back helped me a lot (page 8).

Just as with anything, it's important not to overdo it, pushing music down your throat. Just saturate your ambiance with the sound of the harmonica. And of course, attend live concerts! Nothing motivates you to master any musical instrument as much as a live performance of a person who plays it well.

2. Play by heart more than playing tablature.

Because of the harmonica's design, it is almost impossible to use sheet music for this instrument. This is why one could say that the sheet music has not yet managed to "ruin" the harmonica. Still, there is tablature (we will talk about it in our first lesson). It is very important, once you start learning a melody or lick by tablature (or tab for short), to "tear" yourself away from the music sheet as soon as you can and start play it by heart. Only the melody played by heart becomes alive and starts to convey the range of your emotions. Most importantly, never – yes, NEVER play a melody in front of an audience using sheet music! It's just not right.

3. Picking up by ear more than playing what you've learned from tablature.

Here everything is plain and simple: if you hear a phrase (usually called a "lick") or recall a melody, try and pick it up on the harmonica. Try playing it right away, without searching for tablature (which may not exist for this particular melody). This is the oldest, easiest, and fastest way of transferring musical knowledge from teacher to student, which will never get old. After all, isn't it how we – back when we were kids – learned to speak? We just repeated words and phrases we heard from people around us.

Of course, you will not immediately be able to pick up music by ear. It will take some time. But even a simple lick played in such a way no longer feels strange to you but becomes "yours". Your "musical vocabulary" will begin to expand very quickly. Having mastered picking up music by ear from audio and video sources you will gain access to absolutely all the melodies you hear. Only the possibilities of the instrument will limit you.

4. Improvise more than play ready-made tunes.

This is probably the most basic of the rules. It comes easily to preschoolers, but adults have a hard time with it. Usually this is because back in their school days many adults have been fed scary stories that improvisation is super difficult and close to impossible. That's just not true! Believe me - anyone can improvise! We will start doing it from the very start – and you will be surprised how simple it is!

5. Play for fun.

I guess this should have been the first rule... Never forget why you started learning the harmonica in the first place - to have fun! When something doesn't work out exactly as you'd expect, remember that. Not everything happens just the way we want it to, but there are things we already have and learned to do that give us a reason to be happy.

Don't torture yourself with long practice hours if it feels more difficult that you can handle. You will be much better off practicing the instrument intermittently for 10-15 minutes at a time rather than doing it for an hour and a half – inflicting pain on yourself (and your neighbors!) once a week. Carry the instrument with you in your bag, backpack, or pocket and play whenever you get a chance and (most importantly) when you're in the mood.

One last rule about this self-tutorial. In the book you will see links to audio and video materials. Don't skip over them. Listen and watch every audio and video. Without audio and video the lessons will not do much good.

I think we've been talking a bit too much ☺.

Go ahead and take the harmonica out of the box. Oh, so you've already taken it out? I see.

Is it in the key of C? Is there a C on the instrument and on the box? Perfect! That's exactly what we need. I'll explain what that means a little later.

Right now let's move on to Lesson One!

1. Bob Dylan. Some might say that Dylan may not be your best harmonica player. Then I would ask: Who is better than him at playing folk harmonica, and doing it while playing the guitar? To my knowledge, none among today's world's best and famous players. The sound of his harmonica is truly original, warm, relaxed and yet sincere. He did not always strive to hit the right notes (I would dare to say he rarely if ever hit the right ones), but the warm, country-infused and confident tone of his harmonica have become recognizable all over the world. Bob Dylan is good to listen to if you are afraid to improvise because of the fear of not hitting all the right notes. Listen to Dylan (especially his first two folk albums). He is anything but afraid. The principle "it came out just as it was supposed to" is one of the fundamental principles of improvisation and Bob Dylan mastered it perfectly.

2. Billy Branch is hands down the best blues harmonica player in America.

I don't think there's much more to say about him. He's the best and he's still going strong. Listen to his records. I'd recommend starting with "Double Take". It's a great duet album of him with guitarist Kenny Neal. It shows off Billy's harmonica in all of its glory.

3. Sonny Terry. His trademark fidgety, sort of nervous sound has become the standard for Delta Blues. He recorded most of his songs and tunes with equally iconic guitarist Brownie McGhee. They've been playing together since the 1940s and it would be impossible to imagine them apart. Listen to their duet to get a real esthetic treat.

4. Carey Bell. An outstanding bluesman from Chicago with a good performing technique and some trademark sound "tricks". He has been doing recordings with his son Lurrie Bell on the guitar since the 80's. All the recordings are worth the attention, especially their acoustic album released in 2008.

5. Charlie McCoy The iconic country harmonica player. The man who actually created the modern cross-harp country harmonica sound. A master of country and bluegrass improvisation. After Charlie arranged the fiddle bluegrass tune Orange Blossom Special on the harmonica, the last skeptics had to admit that the harmonica was a real, serious musical instrument.

Of course, that's by no means the entire list! I haven't mentioned Junior Wells, Sonny Boy Williamson, Buddy Greene, James Cotton, and many, many others. To cover them I'd have to write a separate book. So, learn the names of harmonica players you're not familiar with. After all, each one of them has some zest in their playing. The more performers you hear, the richer your performing musical vocabulary will become.

Good luck in discovering your own sound!

PART I

𝄞 FIRST POSITION - TONIC MAJOR 𝄞

Lesson 1

As is always the case, the first lessons start off with some minimal music theory and new terms that apply to our instrument. We'll need all of this later on, so be patient.

Pick up your harmonica.

There are different ways to hold it. Let's not get distracted by that. Let's just take the instrument in the most common and effective way right away. The main holding hand is the left hand. Take the instrument in your left hand, as shown in *Figure 1*. Look closely, the harmonica is actually sandwiched between the two fingers of the left hand - the thumb,

Figure 1

and the index finger. There are usually longitudinal indentations on the top and bottom lid of the harmonica. They are made for easy holding. This is where the thumb and index finger should be placed.

Do you see the numbering of holes 1-10 on the top cover? If you do, then the harmonica is in the right position. If suddenly the numbers are on the bottom, in front of your thumb - turn the instrument over.

The right hand is there for support. It helps holding the instrument and, in combination with the left hand, can create a "sound chamber", which can close and open (*Figure 2*).

Now let's make the first sounds on the harmonica. You need to know that the harmonica is a wind reed instrument. To put it simple, it needs a steady and uninterrupted supply

Figure 2

of air so that the metal tongues inside can oscillate and create sound. Hence, it is important to place your lips around the harmonica and just confidently exhale into it. You don't have to blow with all your strength, as if you were inflating a balloon. Just a steady stream of air is enough.

Now that you've tried that you've probably got a few sounds going on at once. That's because you exhaled into several holes at once. Now we're going to learn how to hit only one hole - that's actually the

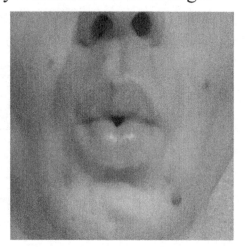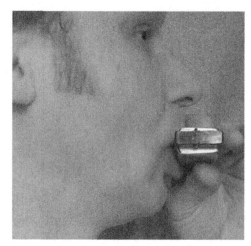

Figure 3

most important task of the first lesson. HITTING ONE HOLE. Without mastering this you can't move on to the second lesson.

The secret of hitting only one hole lies in the correct embrace of the harmonica with your lips. Do not reach for it with your lips and, at the same time, do not push it into your mouth. Simply wrap your lips around the harmonica so that the upper lip is on the top and the lower lip on the bottom lid. Gradually pull your lips into a narrow "tube", as if you were holding a straw with your lips, wanting to drink juice from a small juice pack (*Figure 3*).

It is **_IMPORTANT_** to make sure that the harmonica "lies" on the lower lip. Do not lift it to the upper lip, and do not scuff it upwards. Ideally, the harmonica's holes should point slightly downward. (A detailed and visual demonstration of hitting one hole is shown in the video for this lesson *(Video 2)*).

Video 2

Note: The reason for not being able to hit one hole may be not only due to the shape of your lips, but also due to the position of the instrument relative to the lips. If you hear two sounds played at once instead of the desired one, there is a high probability that you are not in front of the hole, but in front of the bridge between the two holes. The airflow splits into two and two tongues on the neighboring holes sound at once. To eliminate this, just move the instrument slightly left and right to find the correct position.

It is also ***IMPORTANT*** to make sure that your lips do not stick to the face plates of the instrument and slide easily. Lick your lips before you start playing and during the process too (and wipe the harmonica with a tissue when you are done).

Once you've managed to hit one random hole accurately and exhale a sound, do the same with the 1st, 4th, 7th, and 10th holes.

All four of the sounds you got are tonic sounds. That is, they determine the tonality of the instrument. Moreover, they are one and the same sound. In this case, it is the C sound (and on the D harmonica, for example, the same holes will yield the D sound, etc.). As you can see, on the C harmonica we have four C sounds. Each successive one is higher than the previous one. Why do the sounds on any musical instrument, as they rise, repeat? Because they do not rise linearly, but, as it were, in a spiral. It is like climbing a staircase in a multi-story building. Each time, after a certain number of steps you will always find yourself on a floor that is very similar to the previous one, but only higher.

The interval between the two nearest C's is called an octave. As we can see, our harmonica has 3 such octaves: 1-4, 4-7, 7-10. First, we will deal with the main octave - the Center Octave.

Try again blowing into the 4th hole, hitting exactly one note.

Now take a breath! And make sure that only one note is played. Yes - on the harmonica sounds are produced not only when you exhale (it's called blowing), but also as you inhale (it's called drawing).

You got it? Then you're ready to play a scale and this will be the last task for today. We will play a scale in C major since we have a harmonica in the key of C.

It's going to have the following notes: **C - D - E - F - G - A - B - C.**

The way to play it is simple:

4th hole – blow, draw;
5th hole – blow, draw;
6th hole – blow, draw;
7th hole – draw, blow (!)

Let's write it down in tablature *(Track 1):*

4↑ 4↓ 5↑ 5↓ 6↑ 6↓ 7↓ 7↑
C   D   E   F   G   A   B   C

As you have probably understood, the up arrow ↑ is for blowing and the down arrow ↓ is for drawing.

Under each digit is written the letter designation of the corresponding note (it doesn't matter as much when you play, but we will need it later on).

Were you able to play the scale? Great! Now try and play it in the opposite direction - from right to left, from the 7th to the 4th hole.

Practice the scale and start every lesson with it. As soon as you can play the scale nice and clean you can move on to the second lesson.

Lesson 2

Now, let's play our major scale in the upper octave. It will look like this *(Track 2)*:

7↑ 8↓ 8↑ 9↓ 9↑ 10↓ 10↓

C   D   E   F   G   A   C

Track 2

Did you get it? That's great! And now in two octaves. From the 4th to the 10th hole and back *(Track 3)*:

4↑ 4↓ 5↑ 5↓ 6↑ 6↓ 7↓ 7↑ 8↓ 8↑ 9↓ 9↑ 10↓ 10↑

C   D   E   F   G   A   B   C   D   E   F   G   A   C

As you can see, starting from the 7th hole we play the scale first drawing and then blowing. Yet we first exhaled and then inhaled before we reached the 6th hole. That's the design feature of the harmonica, that's how it's made up. This is done so that all the tonic sounds (the C sound, in our case) would be played by blowing. There was no other option but to "flip" the sounds in the 7th and all subsequent holes.

Track 3

___IMPORTANT___ point: Do you have enough breath? When playing the scale, are you already gasping for breath? It is important to realize that breathing on the harmonica is natural, during the playing, via mouth, largely because we play by both drawing and blowing. This way your breathing is regularly alternated. BUT! The oxygen supply is restored through drawing by mouth by about 70%. We supply the remaining 30% via nose. For example, if we do not have enough air, then at the next inhalation in a melody or a scale, we simultaneously draw with our nose. And if, on the contrary, the lungs are already full, then with the next exhalation we simultaneously get rid of the excess air through the nose. That is, when playing the harmonica, our nose is an additional air "valve", which is included in breathing only if necessary.

Also, you probably noticed that the upper octave scale is not full. There's a sound missing. In the upper octave, the next to the last note of the scale, the B, is missing. That sound had to be sacrificed because it didn't fit into a ten-hole harmonica. You'll find out later that this is not the only note missing from our instrument.

Well, it's time to play our first tune! Let's take something really simple and familiar.

How about **"Twinkle, Twinkle, Little Star"**? It goes like this:

4↑ 4↑ 6↑ 6↑ 6↓ 6↓ 6↑   5↓ 5↓ 5↑ 5↑ 4↓ 4↓ 4↑

6↑ 6↑ 5↓ 5↓ 5↑ 5↑ 4↓

6↑ 6↑ 5↓ 5↓ 5↑ 5↑ 4↓

4↑ 4↑ 6↑ 6↑ 6↓ 6↓ 6↑   5↓ 5↓ 5↑ 5↑ 4↓ 4↓ 4↑

That's the tablature (or tab for short). And now, using our first melody as an example, I will give you an algorithm for learning any songs and melodies quickly and correctly, which will come in handy in the future:

Track 4

1. First, listen to the melody several times (use the lesson audio guide). When you listen for the last time, look at the tablature, making sure that the notes of the melody played are written on the paper *(Track 4)*.

2. Play the melody using the tablature. Play slowly at first in a tempo that you feel comfortable with. (I want to emphasize that the tablature is a kind of a "cheat sheet", with the help of which we find the sounds we need on the instrument in the correct sequence. However! Tablature does not convey the rhythmic pattern of the melody and the duration of individual notes. Both the duration of sounds and the melody pattern must be memorized as you listen to it). If something sounds strange and you feel you've lost the melody, go back and listen to the track again.

3. Learn the melody well and play it from memory. It's easiest to break the melody into smaller parts, memorize them and then put them together. I recommend memorizing licks and lines. That way you won't lose the integrity of the piece. But if you keep stumbling over some lick or note while playing, you should work out this part of the melody separately and then put everything together again. Do not leave those difficult spots for later, don't practice the mistakes!

4. Play the melody with the accompaniment, which is also included in the audio appendix to the lesson. At first, the sound of the guitar may throw you off, so feel free to play using tablature at first. But only when you play everything by heart, you can say that you have completely mastered the melody.

5. Don't despair if something doesn't work right away. After all, it's just a melody - that's all. If it didn't happen today, it will happen tomorrow. Don't forget to take breaks and rest. Believe me - it's no less important than practicing!

And one more thing. Lessons are put together by topic. They also go from easy to more difficult. Some can be completed in as little as an hour, and some may take several days. Keep that in mind.

Have fun mastering scales and melodies. I look forward to seeing you again in Lesson 3!

Lesson 3

In this lesson, we'll learn two new tunes, discover a couple of playing techniques, and, at the end, try our long-awaited first improvisation!

As I said above, the goal of this book is to teach you how to improvise. However, playing well-known tunes is also an important element of learning. It disciplines you, develops the necessary minimum amount of diligence (which is often lacking in male students), and gives you the joy of the first tangible results. Playing the harmonica becomes neat, structured and meaningful. So let's not completely give up playing melodies, especially at the initial stages.

First, let's play an old French melody **"Frère Jacques"** ("Brother John") *(Track 5)*:

4↑ 4↓ 5↑ 5↑ - repeat

5↑ 5↓ 6↑ - repeat

Track 5

6↑ 6↓ 6↑ 5↓ 5↑ 4↑ - repeat

4↓ 3↑ 4↑ - repeat

The entire melody consists of just 4 licks, each of which is played twice. (I've intentionally written the melody in shorthand, not duplicating the licks with tablature. Get used to abbreviating so that you don't get distracted by that extra writing).

In general, repetition of phrases is a common phenomenon in music, especially in folk music. You will encounter it regularly when playing melodies.

> ***IMPORTANT!*** Do your cheeks start to hurt when you play? If they do, it means you're straining them. You don't have to do that. We put our lips together in a "tube" shape but our cheeks are always relaxed (!). When we exhale, they puff up slightly, and when we inhale, they retract. Follow this. Play around in front of a mirror to make sure your cheeks are "breathing".

Here's another well-known piece from the United States. It's a traditional black gospel tune **"Oh When The Saints Go Marching In!"** *(Track 6).*

4↑ 5↑ 5↓ 6↑ - repeat

Track 6

4↑ 5↑ 5↓ 6↑ 5↑ 4↑ 5↑ 4↓

5↑ 5↑ 4↓ 4↑   4↑ 5↑   6↑ 6↑ 5↓

5↓ 5↑ 5↓ 6↑ 5↑ 4↑ 4↓ 4↑

Now let's turn to a couple of playing techniques that will introduce you to the most common types of harmonica articulation strokes.

1. Staccato is a type of articulation where the sounds are played in a short, brisk manner. In sheet music or tabs, a sound played staccato is marked with a dot (drawn above or below the note).

To achieve a staccato sound, we will need the active help of our tongue. Let's try to play a staccato on the blowing in the fourth hole. To do this, we need to whisper "TOOT" as we exhale. As we pronounce the letter "T" our tongue works like an air valve, which first accumulates air, blocking its exit from the mouth, and then sharply releases the air. As a result, we hear the letter "T". On the harp, if the tongue returns to the original position of the letter "T", we get a short, staccato sound. If you don't return it, you get "Tu-u-u-u", i. e., a long sound with a sharp, distinct beginning *(Video 3).*

Video 3

Now try playing staccato as you draw. It's very similar. At first it may not feel as natural to pronounce a consonant letter on the draw, but it's really not that much harder to get used to it.

Track 7

Now let's play a staccato scale from the 4th to the 7th hole. In order to hear something, we'll play 4 identical staccato notes in a row instead of one *(Track 7)*

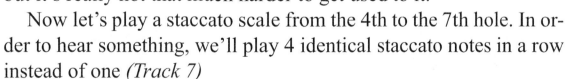

4̇↑ 4̇↑ 4̇↑ 4̇↑ 4̇↓ 4̇↓ 4̇↓ 4̇↓ 5̇↑ 5̇↑ 5̇↑ 5̇↑ 5̇↓ 5̇↓ 5̇↓ 5̇↓ 6̇↑ 6̇↑ 6̇↑ 6̇↑

6̇↓ 6̇↓ 6̇↓ 6̇↓ 7̇↓ 7̇↓ 7̇↓ 7̇↓ 7̇↑ 7̇↑ 7̇↑ 7̇↑

Once you are able to play a staccato scale, it is safe to say that you got the feel for this stroke.

The opposite of staccato is legato. The "legato" sounds flow smoothly from one to the other.

The harmonica is a melodious musical instrument that naturally leans more toward legato. Excessive use of staccato sounds can make your playing feel jaggy, scratchy, and even unpleasant to the ear. But without staccato the harmonica loses its playfulness and fire. Moreover, you just wouldn't be able to play several identical sounds in a row in a moderate to fast tempo without staccato... so we will use this stroke but use it wisely.

2. Slide is just that - sliding on the instrument. A signature technique, without which it would be difficult to imagine the harmonica.

Slides are made both on blowing and drawing. There are two types of slides:

I. Slide proper - this is when we slide the harmonica (blowing, or drawing) from bottom to top, or from top to bottom from some **undefined hole,** but definitely stopping at **a specific one.** Basically, we slide toward a sound from above, or from below. Here it is important to make sure you play this sound clean – then you can say the slide is successful.

II. Dropoff - we make such slides from a specific, already sounding note. We let it sound, and then slide "toward nowhere", i. e., without a definite ending note. This is usually done at the end of a melody, or solo.

For more information about slides, see the video for this lesson *(Video 5).*

Video 5

Guess what? It's time for **your first improvisation!!!** Yes, the time is now, even though you may not feel like you're ready. But you either do it now, or you never will.

For starters I've got to tell you the most important improvisation secret that you won't hear anywhere else. Hence, **_ATTENTION!_** You need to turn on the music track you've picked for improvisation (it's in the video attached to this lesson), take your harmonica in your hands... and start **playing anything!!!!** Yes, anything. Just move your harp, while changing breaths. Do slides and staccatos wherever you want to. Play the sounds and enjoy hearing the result. That's real improvisation - **when you start playing and you don't know what you're going to get.** The main thing is to try to make it beautiful. For that you just need to hit the random notes so that they sound clear. Even if half of the sounds turn out to be double or triple - it's no big deal. It is not always necessary to hit and play one note at a time. It is **<u>IMPORTANT</u>** not to be afraid to make mistakes. Taking a wrong note on the harmonica is actually almost impossible, because it is a diatonic instrument, i. e., simply put, it is a one-scale instrument. If the key of the song corresponds to the key of your harmonica (and in the appendix to the lesson everything corresponds exactly), it is simply impossible to make a mistake. All the sounds on the harmonica are those that exactly match.

All right - one more, final prep. I call it "The Chaotic Scale."

Play the harmonica, moving from the 1st to the 10th hole, changing your breath as if you were playing a scale, but quickly and without thinking about which holes you're hitting. Just blow, draw, blow, draw, draw, blow, draw... and so all the way up to the 10th hole *(Track 8)*.

1 ↑↓↑↓↑↓↑↓↑↓↑↓↑↓↑↓↑↓ 10

Track 8

Great! So now you've learned how to change your breathing to play at random. You're definitely ready. Watch the video and have a great time doing your first improvisation! *(Video 10)*

Video 10

Lesson 4

Let's look at a couple more new melodies that are written in ¾ time signature. Simply put, it's your "waltz signature". "Oom-pah-pah, oom-pah-pah." Don't lose the time signature when you play melodies.

Let's start with a German folk song, which has probably been played on the harmonica since the early days of this instrument. It would be wrong to pass it by.

1. **"Oh, My Dear Augustin"** *(Track 9)*

6↑ 6↓ 6↑ 5↓ 5↑ 4↑ 4↑ 4↓ 3↑ 3↑ 5↑ 4↑ 4↑

6↑ 6↓ 6↑ 5↓ 5↑ 4↑ 4↑ 4↓ 3↑ 3↑ 4↑

4↓ 3↑ 3↑ 5↑ 4↑ 4↑ - repeat

6↑ 6↓ 6↑ 5↓ 5↑ 4↑ 4↑ 4↓ 3↑ 3↑ 4↑

Track 9

Once you've gained some confidence playing this melody, try taking the first sound in the first, second, and last lines (6↑) as a slide, and from the last long sound of the melody (4↑) make a dropoff. You'll see how just 4 slides will transform the melody, adding to the German folk sound. The slide is a very expressive device.

2. The second melody will prepare you for the perennial question what to present for your friends' and relatives' birthday – for the whole year! This time you will be able to perform this famous tune *(Track 10):*

"Happy Birthday to You"

6↑ 6↑ 6↓ 6↑ 7↑ 7↓

6↑ 6↑ 6↓ 6↑ 8↓ 7↑

Track 10

6↑ 6↑ 9↑ 8↑ 7↑ 7↓ 6↓

9↓ 9↓ 8↑ 7↑ 8↓ 7↑

Notice the third line, specifically the three blows in a row (9↑ 8↑ 7↑). All three sounds should be played on one blowing, rhythmically moving the harmonica with the correct hole to the lips. Do the same with the next two breaths (7↓ 6↓). This way these sounds will come out smoothly.

Now let's look at a couple more methods of playing the harmonica:

1. Trill. A staple of the harmonica playing technique, this is a rapid alternation of two neighboring sounds, merging into one iridescent, dynamic sound. Since we can play two sounds at once in each hole (one for blowing, the other for drawing), the trill on the harmonica is 2 types:

I. A single hole trill. This is when the sounds alternate very quickly on just one hole. If you would alternate between them using a usual drawing and blowing, you would not get a trill, because it is not possible to change the breath as quickly as it is necessary for a trill. To get it to work, it is necessary to work as if to draw and blow only using your mouth, without involving your lungs. It's a challenge to try and put it into words. It's much easier to show. Follow the link to the video where I explain and show 2 types of trills in detail *(Video 6)*.

Video 6

II. Trill on two neighboring holes. With this type of trill, we quickly alternate between two sounds on the drawing or blowing that are on the adjacent holes. I. e., it is not necessary to change the breaths. You just need to move your head quickly from one hole to another. To do this you need to fix the instrument well in your hands, put it to your lips and very quickly begin to turn your head left and right, as if shaking with your head: "no-no-no" and at the same time make an a blow or a draw. (This trill is also shown in detail in the above-mentioned video).

2. The second technique, or, I would even say, sound effect, which we will deal with in this lesson, is the so-called **"wap-wap" effect.** It's a sound you've definitely heard, especially in westerns and delta blues. With the wap-wap effect, you can emphasize individual stretched sounds, or chords, adding a kind of "weepiness" to them. In westerns "wap-wap" is often played through the whole melody, thus parodying the tremolo harmonica or accordion. In any case, this technique is performed exclusively with the help of our hands. With our palms we create a chamber around the back of the harmonica, which we alternately open and close with our right hand.

Again, this is easier to show, so follow the link to the video *(Video 4)*.

Video 4

As we come to the close of our lesson we will improvise again. This time we will apply all the skills and techniques (slide, staccato, legato, trills and "wap-wap") *(Video 11)*.

Video 11

Lesson 5

This time we're going to start right away with improvisation. I'm sure to some of you it may have seemed a little difficult last time. So, let's go over the improvisation from the previous lesson in detail (*Video 13*).

Video 13

Did you warm up on the improv? Great! Now let's continue to improve our technical level.

Today we'll start by playing the first two melodies from our repertoire ("Twinkle, Twinkle Little Star" and "Brother John") in the upper octave. The last melody we learned, as you remember, is played in the upper octave. But all the others can be **transposed** (i. e., transferred) there as well.

To do this, you just need to start playing them not from the 4th, but from the 7th hole. Nothing else changes. Where there were draws in the melody - there are still draws, where there were blows - there will be blows.

BUT WAIT! There's one catch. Do you remember that from the 7th to the 10th hole, the draws come first when we play a scale? That's an important point. In the upper octave, the draws are shifted one hole forward. This will affect the tunes you will be playing as well. You'll need to make your draws one hole higher than your blows.

<u>For example,</u> let's take the first line of **"Twinkle, Twinkle Little Star."**

We used to play it like this: 4↑ 4↑ 6↑ 6↑ 6↓ 6↓ 6↑. The only two draws in this line were in the same place where the blows were before - on the 6th hole.

In the upper octave, this line is played as follows:
7↑ 7↑ 9↑ 9↑ 10↓ 10↓ 9↑. See? The blows are in the same place as in the main octave (from the first two blows we jump to the other two through the hole, nothing changes here), but the draws are played not above the blows, but one hole higher. And then for the last blow we go down one hole again.

This way, when playing in the upper octave, we need to "correct" for all the draws in the melody by a shift of one hole.

Now try playing melodies in the upper octave. I am purposely not writing out the tabs for you. It is important to me that you do it by ear and by feel, otherwise you will not master transposition. Listen to the audio (*Track 11*) to hear how it should sound. After that, try playing the melody. And REMEMBER - you will make mistakes now and then anyway! I myself almost always make mistakes when transposing a learned melody, but... I correct myself very quickly and no one

Track 11

notices it!

The main trick to playing in the upper octave is to be able to correct yourself quickly. If the sound on the draw sounds off, it means you just played it lower than you should. Quickly move one hole up and no one will notice the mistake, because the mistake will turn into a beautiful micro-slide.... That's just a little tip from me.

"Brother John" will start the same way with a blow in the 7th hole. Then draw at the 8th hole... then you can take it from there. Here's the track: *(Track 11a)*.

Track 11a

The new playing technique we're going to start learning today is vibrato.

Vibrato is an oscillating change in the volume (strength), or pitch, or tone of the sound of an instrument, as a result of which we hear a sound vibration or oscillation.

What is vibration used for anyway? The point is that long, bland sounds are hard on our ears since they are monotonous. But when you add a little vibrato to the same long sound, you can listen to it for hours and not get tired. That's our physiology. We perceive vibration in sound as something pleasant, weighty, convincing, expressive. Yes, vibration is a very expressive technique that can turn the simplest melody into a masterpiece (and I am not exaggerating).

Vibration is used in almost all musical instruments where possible. There are instruments on which it is not technically possible, such as a grand piano or a piano. Some instruments are capable of than one kind of vibrato, some can be vibrated in two or even three ways. The harmonica, in this respect, is the most perfect instrument. There are at least 4 ways to do vibrato (and maybe more). I use only three, which I will share with you:

1. Hand vibrato (performed exclusively with the hands);
2. Breath vibrato;
3. Throat vibrato.

In this lesson, we will talk only about the first type of vibrato.

1. There are two types of **hand vibrato:**

I. Left hand vibrato. This is the basic vibrato. It sounds soft, clear and its speed is easy to control and change, because the left hand just holds the instrument.

To vibrate the sound in this way, do a steady, long blowing into any hole (for example, the 4th hole) and, as you do, start swinging the harmonica with your left hand so that its holes "roll" onto the lower lip (on the inside of the lower lip). Each time you lower the harmonica downward, during this rocking, the harmonica will sound quieter, and when you return to the initial position, it will go back to the initial volume. The contrast in volume will give you that sense of vibration.

This happens because as you move downward, the hole from which you are currently drawing the sound is partially blocked by the inner, slightly inverted side of the lip. At this point, less air enters the harmonica and it sounds quieter. When returning to the initial position, the air flow to the sounding tongue in the harmonica hole is restored and we hear the sound with the same initial volume.

Again, in practice everything is much easier and clearer than on paper, so follow the link to the video, where I talk about all kinds of vibrato, and provide a more detailed analysis of vibration with hands *(Video 7)*.

Video 7

II. Right hand vibrato. This type of vibrato was very much favored by Sonny Boy Williamson II. Watch his live performances from the 50s and 60s.

The instrument, when using this type of vibrato, remains in the left hand, but the right hand rests on one (usually, middle) or several fingers on the back of the harmonica. Using small, jerky movements we begin to push it toward the lips. The result is a sort of jittery, small-range vibration. It's not suitable for lyrical pieces and beautiful extended notes, but it's just right for adding jittery bluesy tension to the sound of the instrument. Learn more about this kind of vibrato in *Video 7*.

Finally, after practicing vibrato on drawing and blowing on different holes, it's time to apply it to improvisation. Follow the link *(Video 12)*. See you soon at the next lesson!

Video 12

Lesson 6

There is not much theory in this lesson, since it will be more of a follow-up from the previous lesson about **transposition** and **vibrato,** in which we have already discussed the basic theoretical points. So, less words and more practice!

I. Let's transpose 2 more of our tunes into the upper octave, keeping in mind the need to adjust for breath shifting:

Track 12

"Oh, When The Saints Go Marchin' In!" We start with the 7th hole, then blow into the 8th, and then try going on your own, checking with the audio track *(Track 12)*.

"Oh My Dear Augustin" will start in the upper octave with blowing into the 9th hole, then drawing into the 10th (because of the shift) and blowing again into the 9th..... then try again on your own. The first phrase in this melody will be more difficult to play in the upper octave because of the displaced breaths, but this is a temporary, manageable difficulty. So, listen to the track *(Track 13)* and play.

Track 13

II. We will devote the second part of the lesson to **breath vibrato.**

The main idea here is that we put air into the harmonica when we blow (or inhale as we draw) in a wave-like manner, i. e., stronger and weaker. This causes the instrument to sound quieter or louder and we hear the vibration.

Try doing vibrato as you blow first, for example, in the same 4th hole. Start the blowing and in the process try to increase and decrease it in waves. IMPORTANT! make sure that only the diaphragm is used in this "pushing" of the air flow. We use the upper part of the abdomen (diaphragm) to push the air in waves. We do not squeeze the air flow with our throat and do not do anything with our hands. Only breathing, only the diaphragm.

After you get a feel for vibrato on the blowing, do it on the drawing. You can find out everything about this type of vibrato in the video *(Video 8)*.

Video 8

I hope that you got it! In general, vibrato, as well as trill, are techniques that need to be practiced separately. Take some time, sit down and work on them. You won't be able to master expressive playing techniques overnight. But neither do you need to sit long hours, honing them to perfection. As soon as you sense that it's starting to come together, immediately put it into practice. Let's go to the familiar video, where we improvised the first kind of vibrato. Now let's work on perfecting the second vibrato kind *(Video 12)*.

Video 12

I'll give you one more hint about vibrato. When you're playing along, the tempo of the vibrato should be faster than the tempo of the music. The vibrato seems to be a little ahead of, overtaking the tempo of the tune, or instrumental piece you are playing. This is an important point. If the wave-like "beating" of the vibration coincides with the tempo of the piece, the vibrato will turn into separate, rhythmic less-than-sounds. Pay attention to this when listening to how I and other musicians perform vibrato and try to do the same.

Good luck and see you at the next lesson!

PART II

§ THIRD CROSS-POSITION - DORIAN MINOR §

Lesson 7

The next three lessons will focus primarily on the 3rd cross position on the harmonica, the position of the Doric minor.

It is worth clarifying here that the harmonica has three basic positions:

I. The First, aka Major, Position. All the previous lessons were devoted to it. We played in the key of C major which coincided with the tuning of our instrument. All songs and improvisations were in this key. This position is used for playing simple melodies in major keys in folk and country music, German and any other European folk music.

II. The Second Position, or blues position. In this position we play blues (major key blues), country, funk, rock, rock and roll. This position on the harmonica is also called "second cross-position", because the tones of the piece of music and the harmonica used in it do not coincide. In particular, the "C" harmonica can be used to play pieces in the "G" key. We will discuss this in the third part of the book.

The second position is probably the most used, the most popular of all. I'm sure that you too have picked up the harmonica after hearing it played in this cross-position. But, of course, as attractive as it is, it's also difficult to master. That's why we'll take it up after we've learned the third position, which is much easier to learn.

III. The Third Position, sometimes referred to as the position of the Doric minor, or the "third cross-position". It is used to play sad, minor melodies, as well as minor blues, Celtic and Scandinavian music.

It is quite logical to learn the minor keys now, after becoming acquainted with the major, in which we played all the previous tunes. This is also appropriate since the lesson is not that difficult and we will not spend much time on it. On the other hand, unlike many players, we will get access to all minor key pieces! Many folks who take up the harp, get bogged down in the second position and never get to reach the third.

Let's start by playing the Dorian minor scale. It will immediately plunge us into a minor mood, which, I am sure, will surprise you very much. You'll think, "How can such a cheerful instrument weep so sad?" It can do it! It's just one step from sadness to joy. And in this case, just one tone. The Doric scale starts, like any major key scale, on the 4th hole, but not with blowing, but with drawing, starting with the D key. Take a look *(Track 14)*:

4↓ 5↑ 5↓ 6↑ 6↓ 7↓ 7↑ 8↓
D   E   F   G   A   B   C   D

Track 14

It turns out that we play the Doric minor scale on the "C" harmonica in the D minor key. Accordingly, the minor pieces that we can play on our harmonica will also be a tone higher than the instrument, in the key of D minor.

Play the scale through several times from the 4th to the 8th hole and back again. The main sounds of the scale, which set the tonality, the minor sound (played together, they form a minor chord), are on the draw. Play them separately:

4↓ 5↓ 6↓ 8↓   8↓ 6↓ 5↓ 4↓
D   F   A   D   D   A   F   D

This means that when playing melodies and improvisations in the 3rd cross-position, you should "lean" on the drawing rather than on blowing. Most of the licks will begin and end with draws (not all of them, but most of them). To feel it and be certain about it, let's learn an Irish shanty tune about a Drunken Sailor *(Track 15)*:

"Drunken Sailor"

Track 15

6↓ 6↓ 6↓ 6↓ 6↓ 6↓ 6↓ 4↓ 5↓ 6↓

6↑ 6↑ 6↑ 6↑ 6↑ 6↑ 6↑ 4↑ 5↑ 6↑

6↓ 6↓ 6↓ 6↓ 6↓ 6↓ 6↓ 7↓ 7↑ 8↓ 7↑ 6↓ 6↑ 5↑ 4↓ 4↓

⁄6↓ ⁄6↓ ⁄6↓ 4↓ 5↓ 6↓

⁄6↑ ⁄6↑ ⁄6↑ 4↑ 5↑ 6↑

⁄6↓ ⁄6↓ ⁄6↓ 7↓ 7↑ 8↓ 7↑ 6↓ 6↑ 5↑ 4↓ 4↓

As we can see, the melody has both staccato and slides. At the end of the first phrases of each chorus, we play "4,5,6" first on the draw, then on the blow. It is important to play it on one breath, legato (taking a long draw or blow, just moving the harmonica and stopping at the desired hole).

As usual, at the end of our lesson – an improvisation in minor key. Follow the link *(Video 14)* and join me in playing minor key blues.

Good luck! In the next lesson, we'll continue diving into the minor key.

Video 14

Lesson 8

This lesson is almost entirely devoted to a very important harmonica technique, without mastering which we will not be able to play in the 2nd cross position. Even the third minor position would be dull and boring without it, especially when it comes to blues. It's called **a bend.** This is the first time we're talking about it, although I've been using it already in our improvisations.

A bend (on the harp) is a lowering of the sound that we are currently playing, without changing either the breath or the hole. It can sound smooth, drawn-out and have no definite pitch - with such bends we add a sense of sadness and melodiousness *(Track 16)*. But it can also sound quite specific, precise. With such a bend you could play a note that is not initially part of the harmonica, but is needed for a melody or a lick *(Track 17)*.

Track 16

The harmonica bend on the 1st through 6th holes can only be done on the draw, and the 7th through 10th holes can only be done on the blow. Today we're going to look specifically at drawing bends.

In order to make a bend (here let's start again from the 4th hole) *Track 17* you need to hump the tongue, while playing the sound on the draw, so that the tip of the tongue touches the gums of the front teeth of the lower jaw (on the inside, of course), and the "hump" of the tongue formed in this case pressed against the palate, creating an obstacle to the flow of air. This position of the tongue is similar to when we pronounce the letter "h" in the word "here", except that in bending we do a long, long "h-h-h-h-h-h-h" drawing, pursing our lips, lowering the lower jaw and tilting the harp toward the lower lip *(Figure 4)*.

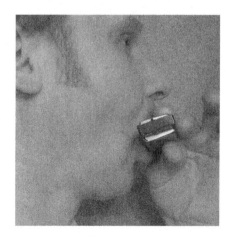

I know this is hard to understand without a video, so watch and repeat *(Video 17)*.

Figure 4

Now make a bend on each hole from the 1st to the 6th. Skip the 5th hole, otherwise you may end up with a broken reed in which case you will have to go looking for another harmonica. First play a clean sound on the draw, then lower it with a bend, then go back to the "clean" sound again *(Track 18)*.

Video 17

(1↓ 1↕ 1↓)   (2↓ 2↕ 2↓)   (3↓ 3↕ 3↓)   (4↓ 4↕ 4↓)   (6↓ 6↕ 6↓)

It takes time to master the bend. Practice it regularly, trying to lower the sound more and more, thus making the bend "deeper". Of course, try putting it to use regularly, particularly in improvisation. Go to the video from the previous lesson and try applying bends on the 4th and 6th holes *(Video 14)*.

Track 18

After that, search on your own for accompaniment tracks in the key of D minor and improvise as well. This will be your first experience of **complete musical independence.** The easiest way to find tracks on YouTube is to simply type in the search box: Blues in Dm, Slow blues in Dm, Funk in Dm, Swing in Dm, Soft rock in Dm and so on. You will discover a huge number of accompaniment tracks in that specific key. You then can practice improvising, using all the techniques of playing from your already impressive arsenal.

Video 14

Good luck!

Lesson 9

Let's do a quick recap of what we've learned so far from all the material we've covered.

In the first part of the book, we…
*   Learned to play in a major key.
*   Figured out the major scale in two octaves.
*   Learned several tunes and transposed them to a higher octave.
*   Got acquainted with such playing techniques as: staccato, slide, two different vibratos, two kinds of trills;
*   Learned the main secret of improvisation and learned its basics.

The only thing is that we haven't touched upon yet is how to play the lower octave scale. But we're about to fix that now.

First, try playing through all the sounds one by one in the lower octave. Here's what you'll get *(Track 19):*

1↑ 1↓ 2↑ 2↓ 3↑ 3↓ 4↑

C D E G G B C

Doesn't sound much like a scale, does it? The F and A notes are missing and G note appears twice.

Track 19

The "bend" technique we learned in the last lesson will help us provide those missing notes and the scale will sound just the way it should *(Track 20):*

1↑ 1↓ 2↑ 2↓ 2↓ 3↓ 3↓ 4↑

C D E F G A B C

Track 20

(Bend on the 2nd hole very deep to make an "F" sound. The blowing in the 3rd hole should be skipped to avoid duplicating the "G" note).

In the reverse scale, you will follow a different order of breathing to make it easier to perform. Here it will be best to play the blow in the 3rd hole, skip the clean draw on the 2nd hole. Basically, after blowing into the 3rd hole, we immediately make a deep bend on the 2nd hole *(Track 21)*:

4↑ 3↓ 3↯ 3↑ 2↯ 2↑ 1↓ 1↑

C   B   A   G   F   E   D   C

Track 21

There you are! Now you know how to play the lower octave scale and we can put it to use, too! By the way, is your draw on the 2nd hole okay? Are you getting a clean sound, or like for most folks, you don't? If you get an unwanted bend instead of a clean note and don't know what to do about it, then this video is for you: *(Video 18)*.

Video 18

Let's add one more thing to your playing and improv skills bank in the major key. I call this trick the **"Looper."** It's a popular trick, which is basically a natural repetition of a spontaneously played phrase. It would probably be long and pointless to describe it on paper - it wouldn't make much sense anyway. Such things should only be shown *(Video 19)*.

In the second, more compact part of this book that was dedicated to the 3rd cross-position, we…

Video 19

- Learned the three most basic positions of harmonica playing.
- Figured out the Dorian minor scale (the most common scale for playing in minor key on the harmonica).
- Learned to recognize where this cross position is used.
- Learned the first melody in a minor key.
- Learned a very important bend technique on the draw and applied it in improvisation. Also, in the current lesson, we applied it to the major scale in the lower octave.

Here's a little more about the 3rd position:

We only played the Doric minor scale in one octave, from the 4th through 8th holes. It doesn't "fit" in the upper octave, but that doesn't mean that we don't use the sounds on holes 8 through 10 in this position. Of course we do! The harp sounds terrific in minor at the top, even though the scale doesn't go all the way to the end. Feel free to play in your minor key improvs using all holes from 4th to 10th.

On the other hand, it would be best to skip going down for now. Though the 1st hole would seem fine, the 2nd and 3rd holes are missing the most important sounds for minor, F and A. Yes, you can "squeeze" them out with bends, but it will sound crooked and squashed, especially against the background of all the other sounds in the scale. So for now just skip going down the lower octave with a minor – not much good will come out of it.

As we round off this summary lesson I want to mention that in some songs or instrumental pieces the key can change in mid-play. This is called **"modulation."** For instance, a song may go up a half step or a step with each new verse. Sometimes it happens only once, usually somewhere before the last verse in the song. What do you do if you're starting to learn this piece? You'll just have to swap your harp on the fly, taking the needed key instrument you prepared ahead of time out of your pocket. If you don't have such a harmonica, then just take a break from playing once you hear a modulation. There's no third option, unfortunately.

But it can also happen that the key alternates, and goes back and forth between a major and a minor, for example. If it's alternating between C major and the parallel Doric Dm, then your harmonica fits right in. In fact, we've played that tune before! It's **"Drunken Sailor."** Remember? The second line in each of its two choruses was in C major.

Now, let's practice that improv with a change of key from C to Dm. We have a special video for that too *(Video 16).*

Video 16

My friend! If you have faithfully completed all the tasks and worked through all the audio and video, then I want to congratulate you – you're already playing the harmonica and you're doing it well! The goal of your training is being achieved. You can already enjoy playing it yourself and make others happy as well. All that's left is learning to play even better by mastering the 2nd cross position. The third part of our book will be devoted to this.

PART III

𝄞 SECOND CROSS ("BLUES") POSITION 𝄞

We have reached the 2nd cross position, more commonly known as the "blues position". In this book, we will primarily deal with the musical and technical component of the blues and blues sound. After all, not all of you may want to play the blues and have to study it only because it is the harmonic and rhythmic basis for almost all popular musical genres and certainly, at least a little bit, has permeated the whole world music. But again, there are those for whom learning to play blues was and still is the main goal. To make the book understandable to a wider audience, I chose to leave the philosophy of blues to your independent study. There is enough literature and movies on this subject. Search it, listen to it, watch it. If blues is really your preferred style, it will find its way to your heart.

Lesson 10

As I mentioned above, the 2nd cross position is why many of you decided to learn to play the harmonica in the first place. It was impossible to master this position right away, because you couldn't even play a 2nd position scale without bends. And the scale here sounds like this *(Track 22):*

2↓	3¢	4↑	4¢	4↓	5↓	6↑
G	B♭	C	D♭	D	F	G

Track 22

As you can see from the first sound, this is a blues scale in the key of G. Yes, **we are playing the G blues scale on the C harmonica.** Consequently, the blues we will be playing will all be in the key of G.

There are only 6 notes in the blues scale, not 7, as we are used to seeing in the other two scales. At the same time, almost all of these notes are played on the draw, two of which are drawn with the help of a bend. That gives us a half step lowering of the sounds B and D to get B♭ (B flat) and D♭ (D flat) respectively. To be able to play the sound lowered by the bend at once, it is necessary to form a "bend position" in the mouth before drawing and only then to draw. You will not be able to get a clean bend of the desired depth at once. You'll need to work on it.

In general, it would be good to practice these two bends separately, and then integrate them into your scale with the help of an electronic tuner. This is a device or computer program for tuning instruments. The tuner can also be downloaded on the Internet as a smartphone app. It will show you exactly what note you are currently playing. Practice taking B♭ and D♭ notes with the tuner and memorize how they sound.

If you get the scale right, you can start playing **blues licks.** Playing licks in 2nd position can help build your technique progress in playing blues. I'll give you several broken down licks in this book. The rest you can pick by ear from the recordings of the musicians you like.

4↓ 4↕ 4↑ 3↑ 3↕ 2↓ *(Track 23)*

2↓ 6↑ 5↓ 4↓ 6↑ 5↓ 4↓ 3↕ 2↓ *(Track 24)*

6↑ 5↓ 4↓ 4↕ 4↑ 3↑ 3↕ 2↓ *(Track 25)*

4↓ 2↓ 4↑ 2↓ 3↕ 2↓ *(Track 26)*

Track 23

Track 24

Track 25

Track 26

In the **1st** and **3rd lick** there is blowing into the 3rd hole. We didn't play it in the scale because it's the same G note as the draw on the 2nd. If it's more convenient to take the G on the 3rd hole in a particular lick, we take it on the 3rd hole. (G is the only sound on the harmonica that is fully duplicated, so that it can be played on both drawing and blowing. That's the way it's used in German folk music. But it helps a lot in blues, too). In the **2nd lick** we have an octave jump (from the 2nd to the 6th hole). We're getting used to that kind of jump. In blues it's the norm. More often even such intervals are taken with a slide. Try it that way too.

The **3rd lick,** in fact, is a reverse blues scale with small changes at the end.

Play these licks until you start to get them right. You don't have to memorize them all by heart. It's enough to load them into our short-term memory, as we did in the **Looper** theme - so that after the first performance by tabs you remember the lick and repeat it without looking at the paper, naturally.

An ***ERROR*** that many people make when playing licks is to memorize them and then try to piece together a sort of "improvisation" out of them. This is not the right way to go about it.. Sure, we can and will use some ready-made blues licks in a solo, especially if we play a famous song and this lick is the main highlight in it. But if you were to play like that all the time... how should I say..... **Combinatorics,** that's what I'd call it. We won't be going in that direction. Let's leave combinatorics to mathematics and analytics, where it belongs. In music, **inspiration** should come first! But it does need some "technical support". That's why we play licks to immerse ourselves in the harmony and sound of the style we are going to improvise in.

At the end of the lesson, we'll look at the **3rd type of vibrato** - throat vibrato. It is also sometimes called "bend vibrato" mainly because of the joint work of the throat and tongue on the drawing. The sound begins to wave downward and we hear the vibration as a result of the contrast of pitch (lower-higher-lower-higher...). However, this effect from the 1st to the 6th hole is obtained only on drawing. On blowing this vibrato is similar in sound to the breathing vibrato, but still has its own specific tone.

This type of vibrato is explained in detail in *(Video 9)*. So, watch the video first.

Video 9

Here we will recap only the basic principles of throat vibrato:

- The wave-like blocking of the airflow is done only with the throat. Neither hands nor breath are helping the throat during this time.

- To create this type of vibrato, you need to rhythmically close and open the throat while blowing (or drawing), as if you were saying a short "ah-ah-ah-ah-ah-ah-ah-ah" (glottal stop). We do this naturally when we cough quietly, sort of in a whisper.

- If, while playing this type of vibrato on the draw, you create a "bend formation" in your mouth, the vibe will become bendy and start to sound blues-like.

Do your best at practicing and I'll see you at the *next lesson!*

Lesson 11

Let's start the lesson by learning how to play a two-octave blues scale. It drops one sound at the top and looks like this *(Track 27)*:

6↑ 7♯ 7↑ 8↓ 9↓ 9↑
G   B♭   C   D   F   G

Track 27

The bend on the 7th hole is tentative, not deep at all, more like a "hint" of a bend. It will not work on the 8th hole, so we just skip the D♭ note – it doesn't exist in the upper octave.

Now let's play a two-octave scale *(Track 28)*:

2↓ 3♯ 4↑ 4♯ 4↓ 5↓ 6↑ 7♯ 7↑ 8↓ 9↓ 9↑
G   B♭   C   D♭   D   F   G   B♭   C   D   F   G

Track 28

Is it completely impossible to do bends in the upper octave?

Not at all! You can and you should do them, but you can only do them from the 7th to the 10th hole on the blowing. That's what we're going to learn now.

This kind of bend is called an **overbend.** We will start from the 7th hole. In order to make a bend on it, you just need to make a bend as you blow!)) It's that simple, isn't it? We "hump" our tongue into the bend position and blow. The only nuance is that this time the tongue "hump" should be closer to the teeth than when playing bends on the lower holes. The position of the tongue is similar to when we pronounce letter "U" *(Track 29)*. Then you just follow the bend rules that you already know. It should sound something like this *(Track 30)*:

7↑ 7♯ 7↑

Track 29   *Track 30*

This bend is hard to hold. The tiniest extra movement of the tongue and it can "slip". That means you may have to sweat a bit before you get it right.

Now let's play an overbend on each hole of the upper octave *(Track 31)*:

7↑ 7↯ 7↑

8↑ 8↯ 8↑

Track 31

9↑ 9↯ 9↑

10↑ 10↯ 10↑   The last bend is usually the hardest.

Practice your overbends. We're going to need them.
And now some more blues licks for you:

2↓ 2↯ 2↓ 3↯ 2↓ 2↓ 2↯ 2↓ 3↯ 3↯ 2↓   *(Track 32)*

⁄5↓ ⁄4↓ ⁄4↑ 3↯ 2↓ 2↯ 2↓   *(Track 33)*

4↯ 4↓ 4↯ 4↓ 4↯ 4↑ 3↑ 3↯ 2↓ 2↯ 1↓   *(Track 34)*

Track 32

Track 33

Track 34

Are you hangin' in there? ☺
Now, let's breathe out and finally improvise the blues!

Starting from the first improv in the 2nd cross position we will continue to get used to being self-sufficient, which is very important when learning. After all, the book will end, but your music-making must continue. I've got to prepare you for that, too! Now you will not just have to play without my prompts, but also you will need to find yourself an accompaniment track in the right key.

Search the YouTube for "Blues in G", "Shuffle in G", "Slow blues in G", "Funky in G". Click on any suggested track and listen to how the harmonica in cross-position blends with the key of G.

The main thing when you play is to forget those licks that you practiced and just play more on the draws, alternating occasionally with blows, of course.... It's all up to you! Ultimately, that's what makes improvisation.

Don't be afraid! No one will criticize you since no one can hear you. Not even me. And most importantly, if you don't hit the right note in your blues scale, you won't miss the blues, because it uses two parallel scales! If you miss one, you automatically hit the other.... Well, that's exactly the subject of the next lesson.

So, play more on the draw and don't think much about anything else.
Good luck!

Lesson 12

As I've already mentioned, the blues uses 2 scales at once. One is the blues scale, and you already know it. The other one is called the **major pentatonic.** This scale has the same tonic (first note of a scale) as the blues scale. It starts on the 2nd hole and goes all the way to the 6th hole and then all the way to the 9th hole. But the pentatonic, as you can hear from the name, has only 5 sounds in an octave. Three of them match the sounds of the blues scale, and the other two do not.

Here is that scale *(Track 35):*

2↓ 3♯ 3↓ 4↓ 5↑ 6↑

G   B♭   B   D   E   G

Track 35

It's not a difficult scale, so once you get it, you can learn it in the second octave, where you don't even need to bend *(Track 36):*

6↑ 6↓ 7↓ 8↓ 8↑ 9↑

G   B♭   B   D   E   G

Track 36

Did you get that? Great! Now combine them into two octaves *(Track 37):*

2↓ 3♯ 3↓ 4↓ 5↑ 6↑ 6↓ 7↓ 8↓ 8↑ 9↑

G   B♭   B   D   E   G   B♭   B   D   E   G

Play this scale to where you have it memorized. Once you've got it down, we can move on to a new pentatonic piece.

Track 37

This will be the classic religious hymn, **"Amazing Grace"** *(Track 38).*

1↓ 2↓ 3↓ 3♯ 2↓ 3↓ 3♯ 3↑ 2↑ 1↓

1↓ 2↓ 3↓ 3♯ 2↓ 3↓ 3♯ 3↓ 4↓

Track 38

3↓ 4↓ 3↓ 3♯ 3↓ 3♯ 3↑ 2↑ 1↓

1↓ 2↑ 2↓ 3↓ 3♯ 2↓ 3↓ 3♯ 2↓

Pay special attention to the lick **3↓ 3♯ 2↓ 3↓**. It occurs three times in the melody and, as practice has shown, it is the trickiest spot,... Practice this phrase separately, then the piece will turn out right.

If you have learned the song, go to the blues licks in which the sounds of two scales are played at once. These are the licks that are used most frequently. I'm sure there isn't a single blues lick in which the harmonica is played only in pentatonic, or only in the blues scale. The pentatonic essentially fills in the harmonica gaps left by the blues scale. The melodic pattern in the lick goes back and forth between the two scales, and the result is a very natural and balanced interweaving of the two harmonies.

2↓ 3↓ 4↓ 5↑ 6↑   5↑ 4↓   4↑ 3↓   2↓ 4↑   3↑ 3♯   2↓ 2↑   2↓   *(Track 39)*

4♯4↓   4♯4↓   6↑   5↓ 4↓   6↑ 5↓   5↑ 4↓   4↑ 3↓   2↓ 4↑   3↑ 3♯   2↓   *(Track 40)*

⟋5↓   5↑4↓3↓   ⟋5↓   5↑ 4↓   4↑ 3↓   2↓ 2♯   *(Track 41)*

Track 39   *Track 40*   *Track 41*

At the end of the lesson, it's time to improvise again. This time I would like to play along with you.

You can use this video, as well as all the previous ones, for all future improvisations in new lessons. I intentionally don't reduce the stock of techniques and use all of them when I improvise. Otherwise, the solos will sound unnatural, school-like. Nobody enjoys such a "solo". It won't make me happy and it won't motivate you to progress. After each lesson, if you wish, review the previously watched videos: listen to my playing, recognize the techniques you already know and try to repeat them. Such repetitions, without tab helps, will occur more and more often. You are starting to break away from following the sheet of paper for good! *(Video 21)*

Video 21

Lesson 13

How are you doing? Did you have a hard time with that last improv? Don't worry about it. I told you I didn't hold myself back on purpose in the video. Now, with each lesson, you'll be able to play more. When you go back to that video, you'll feel that you're already playing better.

In this lesson, we'll look at some of the signature blues licks and **rhythmic riffs** that you can always lean back on and gradually memorize.

What are riffs anyway? A **riff** is a constantly or periodically repeated melodic lick. This lick has a clear, unchanging rhythm and is played in the same tempo. The riff is a kind of a melodic foundation for the beat, the tempo of the piece of music. Everything in the song can change except the riff.

The riff can be transposed up or down with a chord change in the blues (following that chord), but it can also stay the same throughout the whole piece.

There are a lot of riffs on the harmonica and new ones appear every day. We'll look at the most popular and frequently used ones.

4↓ 5↓ 4↓ 5↓ 6↑   It's hard to even count the number of blues songs where this riff is used *(Track 42)*.

2↓ 2↓ 6↑ 5↓ 6↑   Remembering **B.B. King** *(Track 43)*.

↗4↑ 3↓ 2↓ ↗4↑ 3↓ 2↓   You've heard this riff in **"Route 66,"** but it's not just there *(Track 44)*.

2↓ ↗4↑ 3↯ 2↓   Two similar and frequently played riffs *(Track 45)*.

2↓ 4↑ 3↑ 3↓ 2↓   *(Track 46)*

4↯ 4↓ 4↓ 4↯ 4↓ 4↓ 4↯ 4↓ 4↓ 4↯ 4↓ 4↓ 3↓ 2↓

This is a rhythmic phrase rather than a riff, but it serves the same function, except that it does not pervade the whole piece from beginning to end, as riffs do. The phrase begins with four consecutive triplets on the 4th hole **(4↯ 4↓ 4↓).** To make a triplet, it is necessary to draw as if you were going to pronounce the syllables "to-we-tee to-we-tee to-we-tee to-we-tee to-we-tee" *(Track 47)*.

Track 42 Track 43 Track 44 Track 45 Track 46

Track 47 Track 48 Track 49 Track 50

5↓ 5↑ 4↓ 5↓ 5↑ 4↓ 5↓ 5↑ 4↓ 5↓ 5↑ 4↓ 3↓ 2↓

A similar variation. Here the triplet is played on the 5th and 4th holes and each triplet should start with the "tee" syllable to separate them from each other *(Track 48)*.

2↓ 2↓ 3↓ 3↓ 4↓ 4↓ 5↑ 5↑ 5↓ 5↓ 5↑ 5↑ 4↓ 4↓ 3↓ 3↓

(Track 49) And this is a blues bass line. To play it in shuffle rhythm (which is the basic rhythm in blues), you must first play it without shuffle *(Track 50)*:

2↓ 3↓ 4↓ 5↑ 5↓ 5↑ 4↓ 3↓

After that, each note is rhythmically doubled, and then you will get the originally shown bass line.

Let's round off our lesson by learning 4 turnarounds.

A **turnaround** is usually a lick that is often played at the end of a blues square (on the last two bars) and brings us to a new square or a coda.

You may have heard that blues is not made up of verse and chorus, but of identical squares with a standard number of bars. A square is essentially the analog of a verse. A verse just needs a chorus (at least once in a while), while a square does not need one - it is self-sufficient.

As a rule, a square has 12, 16, or 8 bars. There are blues pieces with 9, 11, and 15 bars. But they're rare. The most common form of blues is the 12-bar form. In the last two measures, that's what the turnaround sounds like. (If you don't know what a measure is and don't understand what this last paragraph is all about, don't worry. You can hear when the square ends, right? Well, that's when the turnaround is played as the final phrase in it.)

Let's break down the four popular turnarounds.

The first two are built on the bass line and are played in unison (simultaneously) with the bass:

2↓ 2↓ 3↓ 3↓ 4↑ 4↑ 4↯ 4↯ 4↓ 2↯ 1↓   *(Track 51)*

6↑ 6↑ 5↓ 5↓ 5↑ 5↑ 4↯ 4↯ 4↓ 2↯ 1↓   *(Track 52)*

And a couple of nice, triplet turnarounds.

2↓ 2↓ 3↓ 2↓ 3↓ 4↑ 3↑ 4↑ 2↓ 3↓ 2↓ 2↓ 2↯ 1↓   *(Track 53)*

2↓ 2↓ 3↓ 2↓ 3↓ 4↑ 3↑ 4↑ 4↯ 3↑ 4↯ 4↓ 2↯ 1↓   *(Track 54)*

You will do best to memorize these riffs and turnarounds as well as listen to lots of music (you should be learning to listen carefully, finding familiar licks and turns in other artists' playing). Try again to improvise with the accompaniment and my videos and move on.

Track 51   *Track 52*   *Track 53*   *Track 54*

Lesson 14

In this lesson, we'll explore techniques such as **tongue blocking** and **octave playing.** One of these techniques is derived from the other, so they are forever linked.

To play two or more neighboring sounds on the harp, you just need to wrap your lips around it wider so that the air goes not into one, but into several holes at once....

But what do we do if we need to take a longer interval? For example, to play an octave, i. e., to blow into the 1st and 4th holes at the same time.

(1)(X)(X)(4)

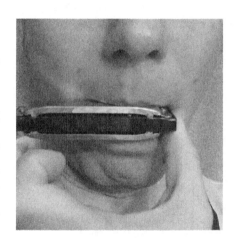

To do this, you need to spread the edges of your mouth wide (as if in a silly smile), plunge the harmonica deeper into your mouth (so much so that when you try to close your mouth, your teeth would bite the lids of the harmonica) and block the 2nd and 3rd holes with your tongue, i. e., just actually plug both of these holes with your tongue *(Figure 5).* In this position, as you blow, the sound will travel along the cheeks through the edges of the mouth into the unblocked 1st and 4th holes and sound an octave *(Track 55).*

Figure 5

Blow and draw into the octave. If you only have one sound, it means you didn't get your lips wide enough around the harmonica. If there are 3, or 4 sounds, then your tongue has not covered the 2nd and/or 3rd holes. Feel with a soft, but also not completely relaxed tongue the two holes at the same time, which it plugs.

Track 55

Octave rarely comes out right away. If it doesn't work, don't despair, keep trying! You have to feel it. Grip the harmonica wide with your lips, raise and lower your tongue. Find the position where the octave sounds best.

If you succeed, play 4 octaves in a row on the exhale, moving the instrument with the right holes. The main thing is that now not just the lips, but also the tongue is sliding on the harmonica.

$$\longrightarrow$$

$$(1)XX(4) \rightarrow (2)XX(5) \rightarrow (3)XX(6) \rightarrow (4)XX(7) \quad \textit{(Track 56)}$$

$$\longleftarrow$$

Now let's play the scale in octaves. A regular major scale. I'll duplicate it here, focusing on the farthest sound on the right of the interval to be played:

$$\longrightarrow$$

$$...4\uparrow \ ...4\downarrow \ ...5\uparrow \ ...5\downarrow \ ...6\uparrow \ ...6\downarrow \ ...7\downarrow \ ...7\uparrow \quad \textit{(Track 57)}$$

$$\longleftarrow$$

The interval that's played using tongue block can also be wider than an octave. It already depends on the width of the mouth and the ability of the tongue to block 3 or more holes. Try to widen and, inversely, to shorten the interval on exhalation and on inhalation *(Track 58)*:

$$\longrightarrow$$

$$(1)XX(4)\uparrow \rightarrow (1)XXX(5)\uparrow \rightarrow (1)XXXX(6)\uparrow \quad \textit{(Track 58)}$$

$$\longleftarrow$$

$$\longrightarrow$$

$$(1)XX(4)\downarrow \rightarrow (1)XXX(5)\downarrow \rightarrow (1)XXXX(6)\downarrow$$

$$\longleftarrow$$

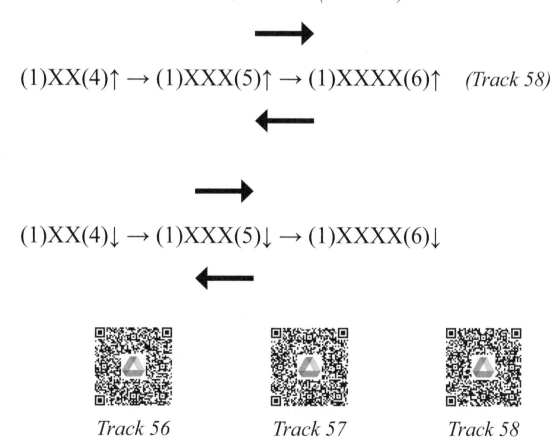

Track 56   Track 57   Track 58

Octave playing is commonly used in rhythmic riffs. Try playing a couple of included samples (they are consecutive in the recording) *(Track 59)*:

(2)XX(5)↓   (2)XX(5)↓ (2)XX(5)↑   (2)XX(5)↑

(1)XX(4)↓   (1)XX(4)↓ (2)XX(5)↑   (2)XX(5)↑

Track 59

(1)XXX(5)↓   (1)XXX(5)↓ (1)XXX(5)↑   (1)XXX(5)↑

(1)XX(4)↓   (1)XX(4)↓ (1)XXX(5)↑   (1)XXX(5)↑

The riffs, moving on the harmonica, easily turn into spontaneous licks. When you play in octaves, you can easily move around the harmonica, changing breaths, doing vibrato, slides and trills - all without breaking the octave shape, the octave "bracket" so to speak.

Here, listen to the track and try to create something similar *(Track 60)*.

Not everything played on the harmonica can even be recorded with tabs. The complex, multi-rhythmic passages written down on paper look visually much more complicated and cluttered than they really are. That's why it's much faster and easier to pick up by ear than to agonize with notation or tablature. I am not saying that paper does not convey the emotional message, expression, recommended tempo, etc. With each new lesson, you need to rely more and more on **your ears** and **less on tabs.**

Now, let's improvise with me using a blues square. The main challenge now, in this improvisation, is to play only octaves! Let's go ! *(Track 61)*

In the next improvisation we will combine octave playing with regular playing, without tongue blocking. The main thing here is to quickly switch from one technique to another. Let's practice it: *(Track 62)*.

Playing using tongue block should be practiced regularly, using it in improvisations and riffs. Yes, in fact, **all the techniques we've learned should be practiced regularly.** That's what we studied them for, isn't it...?

See you at the *next lesson!*

Track 60

Track 61

Track 62

Lesson 15

Listen to these "nasties"! *(Track 63)*

Today we have a "bad boy" lesson! I'll teach you how to make "naughty" sounds and different trademark blues "quips" on the harmonica. After all, blues, like jazz, is full of jarring, sharp sounds, allowing the player to express his emotions, pain and, to an extent, to make himself heard by the listener.

In the first track of this lesson, I took a draw into the 4th and 5th (45↓) holes at the same time and started "fiddling" with this interval using a bend. Then I went down in pairs (34 ↓, 23 ↓, 12 ↓) and also "flattened" them with bends. In general, almost all neighboring holes taken on a draw on the harmonica sound quite sharp. If you add a bend, you will hear the "nasty" sounds. It's like "feeling down in the dumps".

How about this? *(Track 64)* I call it a "fussy bend." Start on the fourth hole. Make a draw with your tongue as if you're saying the letter "U" really fast (U U U U U U U U ...). You'll get a twitchy, bouncing bend. Then be sure to try it on other "bend" holes.

As you'll see, in this track *(Track 65)*, I'm leaning on staccato effects (tuhk tuhk tuhk tuhk tuhk). And some other stuff, like some "fidgety" bends. I just couldn't help myself. Give it a try!

How about this one? *(Track 70)*. I call it "bouncing vibrato." To do this, you need to draw or blow into one or several holes and nervously and rhythmically pull the harmonica away from your lips. In this case, breathing does not stop, and the harmonica "jumps", pulling away from the lips and coming back. It is not difficult, but quite spectacular. Try it!

Let's apply our first "nasty sound" to a lick you already know *(Track 67)*:

4↨45↓45↓ 4↨45↓45↓ 4↨45↓45↓ 4↨45↓45↓ 3↓ 2↓

As you can see, such sounds add some "spice" to your licks and riffs.

Here is a similar lick in the upper octave that looks like there's not much we can do with it. Yet the lick played at the top with overbends always sound very piercing and exciting to the listener *(Track 68)*.

9↨ 9↑ 9↑   9↨ 9↑ 9↑   9↨ 9↑ 9↑   9↨ 9↑ 10↑   10↨

Here we have "frantic hassle" *(Track 66)*. That's the kind of thing that Sonny Terry liked to use in combination with "fidgety bends." We just change our breath very quickly, starting with a draw and move chaotically around the harmonica with a small amplitude. Try it, do it.

As we close this lesson, remember to apply all these tricks in your solos. Boost your playing now with these new techniques putting them into practice *(Track 69)*.

Well, it seems to me that we've done enough mischief for today ☺.

The main thing is to be ready to "fool around" and be mischievous when playing the harmonica, especially when playing blues. It will be fascinating for both you and your listeners.

Let's move on!

Track 63   Track 64   Track 65   Track 70

Track 67   Track 68   Track 66   Track 69

Lesson 16

You know what I noticed? In all the previous lessons, we tended to play almost everything with accompaniment. It's understandable. The harmonica is more of a melodic instrument. You can't play more than two full chords on it. That's why it tends to play along with an instrument that can provide harmony (historically, the guitar) that you can lean on for support.

But the harmonica can be played a cappella (without accompaniment) as well. I'd strongly suggest playing a cappella periodically, solo. Only when you are one-on-one with your instrument and no one distracts you, ONLY in this way you can reveal and recognize its true character. You can hear every nuance, every sob. You can play quietly, listening to the hiss of air passing through the harmonica. You can be alone with the harmonica. Let it play on its own. Solitude – when there's just you and your harp – is the best way to establish the closest contact between you and your instrument. You intertwine your soul with hers and it becomes an emotional extension of you.

Let's just play the harmonica. Spontaneously, jaggedly, or, on the contrary, rhythmically, picking up a random riff.

In general, talk one-on-one with your instrument. Here is a video to help you start *(Video 23)*.

Video 23

Here are some more important solo practice tips. Let's turn on the **looper** in blues position *(Video 20)*.

Video 20

Let's learn how to pick the right harmonica in the right key depending on the key of the songs.

With the harmonica in C, I think you've got it all figured out. You probably remember by now that we use it to play major key melodies in the first position, i. e., in the key of C; also minor key melodies and minor blues in the Dm key; and the major blues, bluegrass and country pieces are in the 2nd cross-position, which corresponds to the key of G.

What about the other harmonies and the songs in other keys? With the 1st position everything is pretty clear. For instance, if a song is in the key of A major, then the harmonica will have to be an A-harp. Key to key. What about the 2nd and 3rd cross-position? Usually, to answer this question, people draw large tables of correspondence of harmonica keys to the songs keys in the three positions. Some manufacturers even print such tables on the harmonica boxes. But I'm not going to do that. I want to teach you how to get along without a table, which rarely if ever is at hand. Usually, it's "right now" that you need to pick the right harmonica and play.

1. The first thing you need to do is remember (or memorize) the alphabet from A to G. Imagine that it is looped, i. e., that after G there is an A again and so on in a loop.

A_B_C_D_E_F_G_A_B_C_D_E_F_G_A

This range of the alphabet letters corresponds to the Latin names of notes and, accordingly, to their key signatures. This designation has been accepted since the first millennium A. D.!

Now let's find out how to match the harmonica to a song in a certain key:

If it's a blues piece, you just need to **count to 4,** going up the alphabet order, and you'll know the tonality of the harmonica. <u>For example:</u> The blues is in the key of A. We count, starting from the song key: A is 1, B is 2, C is 3, D is 4! The key of the right harmonica is "D"!

And so on with any tone in 2nd position. The only thing is, for blues in the key of F, you would need a B♭ (B flat) harmonica (half a tone lower than "B"). I don't want to clutter your head with unnecessary theory as to why this is the case. I'm just sharing with you the simplest practical method, which I have always used and still use, even though I can approach the question in a more complicated way. But why complicate what can be made simple? Count to four and you've got it made!

2. If it is a minor key song, or a minor blues song, you should play the harmonica a tone lower than the song, i. e., corresponding to the previous letter of the alphabet. <u>Example:</u> The song is in the key of Am. In our looped alphabet G comes before A so the harmonica you'd be looking for is G. <u>There are two corrections:</u> For the Fm key we need harmonica E♭ (E flat), and for the Cm key we take B♭ (B flat). This is because the distance between the notes F and E and C and B is only half a tone, and we need to take the instrument a tone lower... But this is only a half-tone correction, which does not destroy the "alphabetic rule".

For a complete picture of the rules for selecting the correct harmonica position, let's look at it from the musical genres perspective, starting with the most fundamental ones:

Folk - in the global ocean of folk, the **harmonica is used in all three positions.** Historically it is used predominantly in 1st (tonic) and 3rd (Doric minor). But it is increasingly common to hear the 2nd cross-position in folk. A lot of things that were once played in the 1st position are now played in the 2nd position, which adds some drive to the melody. We are talking primarily about American folk, Latino, Irish, Scottish, Breton and Scandinavian music.

Blues. Naturally the **2nd position is native to the blues.** But in minor key blues pieces (which are a lot fewer than major blues by comparison) the harmonica is mostly played in the 3rd position. Sometimes the blues is played in the 1st position, in the upper octave, "squeezing out" the necessary blues notes with overbends. Still, the 2nd cross-position is the most important. It's the one that created the signature blues sound.

Country & Western - The 1st and 3rd positions were originally used to play this style, just like with folk. Country songs had more harmonica in 1st position. The more somber minor key Westerns loved the minor harmonica in 3rd position. Today the 2nd cross position has almost completely supplanted the 1st position (thanks in large part to Charlie McCoy and the immense popularity of the blues in the 50s). We'll talk about the basics of fast play in Country music in the next lesson.

Rock and roll, Rock - Almost always **2nd cross-position** since these genres inherited from the blues its harmony.

Pop music is a diverse annual sprout. It is the most variable and includes elements of all genres. The harmonica key will depend on the best resemblance of the genre of the song of interest. I would start picking up the instrument from the 2nd cross position. In one out of two, it's the right one.

At the end of the lesson, we'll improvise again. This time let's play in the Scandinavian style. It's going to be fun!
Check it out in this video: *(Video 24).*

Video 24

Lesson 17

In this lesson we will start (just start, not study in depth) a new long topic called **"harmonica fast play"**. In general, this is a separate skill and a separate tutorial would be necessary that would address fast harmonica playing in **bluegrass** and **country & western music style.** But in this lesson, I will explain to you the basic principles of fast playing. We will try to play some licks and those who are interested in this topic will be able to further study this style on their own. And those of you for whom blues is enough, can enrich your playing with country licks, which is just as great.

The fast play stands on two pillars:
- Microslides
- Rolls

Track 71

Let's take both points apart:

1. Microslides are actually..., microslides)). This is a phenomenon where we play certain sounds in certain sequence sliding between each of these sounds on to the next hole. The breathing doesn't change. We just keep sliding from hole to hole. Let's try to do that *(Track 71):*

4↓→3↓ 4↑→3↑ 4↓→3↓ 4↑→3↑..

And now let's play a major scale using microslides: *(Track 72)*

4↑→3↑ 4↓→3↓ 5↑→4↑ 5↓→4↓ 6↑→5↑ 6↓→5↓ 7↓→6↓ 7↑→6↑

7↑→6↑ 7↓→6↓ 6↓→5↓ 6↑→5↑ 5↓→4↓ 5↑→4↑ 4↓→3↓ 4↑→3↑

A micro slide essentially turns one sound into two consecutive sounds. This allows you to double your playing speed without increasing your breathing rate.

Track 72

2. Rolls are licks that are repeated, "spinning" in the same place. Rolls are **simple** (3, 4, or 5 sounds) and **complex** (made up of several simple rolls, or a combination of simple rolls and common licks).

Let's break down the two types of **simple** rolls.

1) <u>Circular roll</u> - when sounds are looped in a circle:

5↓ 5↑ 4↓→5↓ 5↑ 4↓→5↓ 5↑ 4↓→5↓ 5↑ 4↓...   *(Track 73)*

3↓ 4↑ 4↓→3↓ 4↑ 4↓→3↓ 4↑ 4↓→3↓ 4↑ 4↓...   *(Track 74)*

4↕ 5↓ 4↓ 5↓ 4↕ 5↓ 4↓ 5↓ 4↕ 5↓ 4↓ 5↓ 4↕ 5↓ 4↓ 5↓   *(Track 77)*

Track 73   *Track 74*   *Track 77*

2) <u>Back and forth rolls</u> - when sounds alternate progressively, moving first in one direction and then in reverse sequence *(Track 75):*

4↓ 4↑ 3↓ 4↑. 4↓ 4↑ 3↓ 4↑. 4↓ 4↑ 3↓ 4↑. 4↓ 4↑ 3↓ 4↑...

(the dot between the licks is just for visual separation).

Track 75

Here is an example of a complex roll *(Track 76):*

1↓ 2↑ 2↓ 3↑ 3↓ 2↓ 2↑. 3↓ 2↓ 2↑. 3↓ 2↓ 2↑. 3↓ 2↓ 2↑...

These are just a few examples. There is plenty of rolls and you don't have to memorize them. Moreover, you can invent your own. Try to come up with a few simple rolls.

Track 76

SUMMARY: In the fast play technique, we get the following structure: **Simple rolls** are spontaneously or deliberately "glued" together; when combined with common licks, they create **complex rolls,** which, in their turn, are automatically repeated as much as necessary thanks to our neuron-muscular **"looper".** The latter should be trained to perfection for fast play. Naturally, you should be able to play easily, be able to breathe quickly and literally be able to run all over your instrument. Not straining to hear every sound, nor "savoring" every bend, but to play, play, play enjoying the speed of playing.

This mechanism of fast play is used in country music, bluegrass, Celtic, and to a lesser extent in Scandinavian and Breton music (not because there are no such repetitions there, but because there is not much **fast** play in the last two musical traditions).

All of that was just a quick introduction into the mechanics of this style of playing. Obviously, mechanics alone are not enough. Even if you run faster than everyone else, it will do you no good if you don't understand where and why you're running. Understanding the mechanics doesn't replace the spiritual component of music and inspiration. First, this music must reverberate, pulsate inside of you. To make that happen you need to listen to music a lot, immerse yourself in country and bluegrass tradition. And to listen to it a lot, you need to sincerely love this music... Everything real, creative in our world starts with LOVE! And real music (any kind of music) is no exception to this simple rule. On the contrary, it is the most vivid confirmation of it. Love what you play! Then all the rolls will turn out, and everything else will turn out, and you will not even need tutorial books as much.

Now, as usual, let's improvise together and take an attempt at fast play. It won't be easy, but you've got to give it try. Listen, repeat, try again and don't be afraid. I'll be helping you *(Video 22)*.

Video 22

Lesson 18

This lesson is primarily for those who plan to play the harmonica on stage, or rehearse with a music band. Nevertheless, those who don't plan to do so will also find it interesting and useful.

The topic for today is very practical –
Playing amplified.

Video 25

When you're playing on stage, or with a band, skill and talent alone are not enough. The harmonica, as well as any other instrument in such cases, needs to be properly miked. I explain all of this clearly in two video clips to this lesson. So first watch them carefully, and only then go back to the text *(Videos 25, 26)*.

Video 26

Did you watch it? Great! Now let's summarize briefly:

- The harmonica is miked using exclusively an instrumental, or vocal microphone.
- A standard vocal or instrumental microphone can stand on a microphone stand. In this case it doesn't constrain your hands in any way. You can play as easily as without a microphone. But this option is suitable only for solo performance, or in quiet acoustic ensembles, because you cannot amp the volume of the microphone on the stand. It will start to catch the reflected sound of the harmonica and will start giving you feedback. But you can also hold such a microphone in your hands, pressing it against the harmonica. This will add volume. But holding it is not very convenient and the additional weight in your hands will make your movements more awkward.

Special harmonica microphones are of **two main types:**

- **1) Wireless** - the microphone is attached onto a special ring on the left hand finger, it weighs next to nothing and does not restrain movements.
- **2) Bullet-shaped** - these are the traditional blues microphones. They are heavier than wirless, but have a very comfortable shape, beautiful exterior, volume control knob and reduced frequency range, compared to conventional microphones, so they rarely will create feedback. If you connect a bullet microphone to a guitar combo amplifier (preferably a tube one) you can get the signature Chicago Blues sound.
- A cheap alternative to the classic "bullet" mics can be a household, metal

retro microphone for tape recorder. It won't have a volume knob, but it sounds very good with a guitar amp.

- Let me say a few words about all sorts of special effects pedals and processors that try to include microphones. The harmonica doesn't like them very much. The only thing that's good for it is some gain and reverb, and nothing more. Delay and tremolo effects don't work at all with harmonica. But you can experiment. No one can say "no". Maybe you'll find something that will suit your goals.

What do I use? I don't make any secret out of it.

I have two bullets: **Hohner Blues blaster** and **Shure Green Bullet.** I also have a **Suzuki MC-100** and an old microphone for a tape recorder from 1966 **"Octave MD-44".** I connect them to a Canadian 40 Watt **Traynor** guitar tube amp. I'm fully satisfied with such a set.

But you have to search your own sound, and you will surely find it. So good luck with your search!

Conclusion

Well, this book has come to a close. Along with it we've arrived at the end of our immersion into the world of music and the harmonica. I will no longer lead you by the hand through musical styles, harmonies and licks. You'll go on your own. I've given you all the background you need. I didn't have this knowledge when I first picked up a harmonica almost 25 years ago. And there was no internet back then, no decent books available. But there was a burning desire to learn to play and a love of music! The desire and love were enough to help me become a harmonica player. May these two motivators become the most important motivators in life for you too!

Search for your sound when playing the harmonica. Find your favorite performers and listen to them playing and interviews with them. Look for new licks and melodies and learn them, because I have given you only the bare minimum, in part because there are certain restrictions on the use of other people's work. But they don't apply to you as students. Play whatever you hear, whatever you want.

We have not covered everything, because it is not possible to cover everything in one book. For example, we haven't covered topics such as:

The natural minor. It is rarely used, because it is very uncomfortable when playing the harmonica using the standard Richter tuning. However, if you rebuild your instrument in Paddy Richter tuning (or if you buy a harmonica already tuned this way), you can easily play in natural minor. Many Western and Irish tunes will become available to you, half of which can only be played on a harmonica in Paddy Richter tuning.

4th cross-position. Believe it or not, there used to be such a position. It was used in old Westerns well into the 50's. Nowadays even many famous harmonica players and teachers don't know about this cross-position. The essence of it was that the harmonica in C was used in the F key. Yes, it can be played this way too, although it is not usual and not quite convenient. But there are tunes that can be played and sound good only in this position.

German folk, double-stop playing. This style of playing lost its relevance long ago and was forgotten even in Germany, but I was able to recover this technique of playing, for which the standard harmonica tuning was originally developed.

Playing with a holder. This is the skill of playing two instruments at the same time: guitar (most often) and harmonica. A **holder** is a special device, a clamp that holds the harmonica instead of your hands. It is worn around the neck and fixes the harmonica right in front of your mouth, freeing up your hands to play another musical instrument: guitar, piano, even drums (as an option). I personally play guitar in half of my performances and use a harmonica holder, as you have already seen in the instructional videos for this book.

We have intentionally left these topics out so that you don't get confused and have a good grasp of the basics of the three basic positions. Therefore, first thoroughly study what you already have learned, and then try something new on your own. Although who knows, perhaps I'll think about writing a sequel... Your reviews will definitely encourage me to do so ☺.

The harmonica keys tip: Eventually, if you plan to continue practicing the harmonica seriously, you will have to acquire all keys, ALL 12! But for now, you can just start with the basic "three" instruments - **C, D and A.** You already have the first one. If you get two more, you will be able to cover at least thirty-five percent of all tunes and blues pieces!

Where and with whom to play: Play at home with accompaniment, playing along with recordings of your favorite artists, with friends or even with yourself, using a holder (if you play guitar, of course).

I also recommend attending "Blues jams". At first just go, watch and listen to others play, and then join the jammers too. After all, "the best rehearsal is the performance." (For those who don't know, a blues jam is a musical event where musicians of varying levels get together and improvise together. These evenings are held, most often, in music clubs in almost all cities that have clubs at all.)

LS Track

Lastly, I'll share with you a couple of my works that you can play along with:
Last Sunny Day. It's a lyrical pop bluegrass song in the key of G, so it should be played in 2nd cross position, leaning more on the major pentatonic. Follow the link and join me in playing it together *(Last Sunny Day Track)*.

Fastmover. This is an instrumental blues-funk thing in A, so you will need a D harmonica for it. Also, in the second part of the piece there are two modulations: first a step, and then another half step up. So you'll need two more harmonicas, E and F. But if you don't have them, you can just sit back and listen, getting the feel of the playing style and sound *(Fastmover Track).*

F Track

<u>*Good luck, friends!*</u> I had so much fun creating this book and sharing my knowledge with you. I hope you had fun as well. You're off on your own musical voyage. I wish you a fair wind, seven feet under the keel and... see you again soon! ☺

All videos (Playlist)

All videos are also in the same playlist on YouTube* *(online):*

or use the link:

cutt.ly/Vw9sw158

*Turn off YouTube's embedded subtitles. **Click once here.**
These automatic subtitles should not be there.
There should only be subtitles at the bottom that are already embedded in the video.

All audio + videos (Download files)

All audio and videos are also available on Google Drive:

or use the link:

cutt.ly/Dw9swX5I

Important! Be sure to download all files from Google Drive to your computer. We did have a glitch in our system once and our files were temporarily unavailable online. It would be best to download them all at once so you have offline access to them anytime.

Help: albinaopen@gmail.com

ISBN: 979-8361128570

ASIN: B0BKYHL7PC

Learning to play your favorite songs on the piano is easy!

Today the piano is pobably the most popular musical instrument in the world. Playing this instrument will give you an unforgettable experience.

The book contains musical theory, practical exercises, and 65 popular songs for adults.

The author of the book, Avgusta Udartseva, is a close friend of mine, and so I can wholeheartedly recommend to you her book for learning the piano!

United States

United Kingdom

Canada

ISBN: 979-8386419004

ASIN: B0BXMX7ZVN

- Learning step by step: starting with more simple tunes, then gradually moving to more complex songs;
- Includes music theory, instrument history, practice, recommendations and many entertaining songs;
- Learn the position of the body and hands, how to breathe properly and play easily;
- Letters above each note and simple explanations;
- Convenient large US Letter print size;
- Video accompaniment to all lessons by direct link inside the book;
- 2-in-1 Book: Recorder lessons and video + 60 Songs.

United States

United Kingdom

Canada

And it's great for adults

Printed in Great Britain
by Amazon

46410021R00037